Dylan's Battle

Dylan's Battle

By Harry Mitchell

Dylan's Battle

Dedicated to my beautiful mother Emma Mills

My gorgeous fianceè Lucy Faulkner

My favourite people nanny Judy and nanny Jen

I love you all millions x

Dylan's Battle

Chapter One 8am Dylan

21st of September 2023

I'm standing in the middle of my bedroom, I stare in front of the mirror, in my white boxer shorts my nan bought me for my birthday, looking for anything in this room that can kill me. My gut instinct is that I need to end my life. He is telling me I need to end my life, my mental health has been torturing me for far too long now, and I don't know what I am supposed to do. I'm unsure if I have slept in the past 24 hours. All I remember really is the mirror showing me every flaw I have, it insists on telling me how weak I've become. I remember staring at the scars and cuts going up on my arm, and him. He is there wherever I am, he is with me wherever I go, wherever I look, I feel his eyes creating a hole into the back of my skull. The only person who has been keeping

Dylan's Battle

me semi-sane is Chloe, she has been my girlfriend for just over 2 years now, she's the light of my life. She has beautiful long blonde hair, and these piercing blue eyes. She has lips so full you can't stop looking at them until you know you're about to kiss them. She has a laugh so contagious with those pearly white teeth visible every time she laughs.

As my eyes remain transfixed onto the mirror, I look at my own reflection, unsure if I really want to look behind me because I know he is there, he is always there talking to me, I know no one else can hear him or see him, but he seems so real to me, I haven't told anyone because I'm too scared. No one will believe me or they will just try and take me to a hospital full of crazy people and I cannot be going there. **That's where you belong though**

Dylan's Battle

Dylan, because I will fucking kill you. I look over to the figure of the man standing there who has just whispered that to me, I run my hands through my mousy brown hair and start screaming 'fuck off fuck off fuck off, you're not even real so why can I fucking see you' **Dylan you will never escape me, and if you do, people will come looking for you, they will take you away, they will hurt Chloe.** I sit on the floor feeling so defeated, not sure on what to do, unsure of when the last time I slept was. It certainly couldn't have been for very long last night as he was in the room with me talking all of his normal shit. **Stay awake Dylan, you'll die, Chloe will die, you'll lose fucking everything.** Tears start to fall down my cheeks, my heart is beating so fast I can feel beads of sweat forming on my forehead. I sit down in the middle of my bedroom, surrounded by the things I

Dylan's Battle

love, the things I keep, the things that make me feel safe. The concert posters, the photos of Chloe and I, but all of that seems irrelevent, or like a distant memory now. This room doesn't even feel like it belongs to me. I'm trapped in my own home but feel like a stranger intruding. So all I feel I can do is scream, to the point where I feel my throat become red raw, just like I've swallowed 10 razor blades and the taste of blood is running down my throat. I cry, I wonder how the fuck I got here, my whole family abandoned me when my nan passed away. Nan left the house to me in her will, after that my mother and father gave me an ultimatum; either I sign over the house to them or they cut ties with me for good. I knew what I wanted to do, but I also needed to think about my future as my relationship with my family has never been exactly stable. I don't really understand why my family

Dylan's Battle

reacted the way they did, it turned bitter pretty quickly, my mum called me every name under the sun. 'you're no son of mine'. Dad obviously stuck with mum, while giving me a subtle nod. Even though as a family our relationships were extremely rocky, I really miss our good times, I miss mum's cooking, I miss dad watching the football review shows on Saturday morning with the strong smell of black coffee that would take your breath away in the morning. I really fucking miss my mums hugs.

As I think about all of the decisions that have led me to where I am now, the continuous noise that fills inside my mind seems to be getting louder. **You fucked up Dylan, you always fuck up, and now look where you are, fucking useless**. I try to stand up to put my red t-shirt on and navy joggers, but it's just so hard to focus on anything when all you can hear is him '**Why are you putting them on, you look stupid putting them on, no one cares enough to look at you anyway so you may as well stay inside and feel FUCKING SORRY FOR YOUR SAD LITTLE LIFE'** leave me alone leave me alone, tears streaming down my face, I curl up on my bedroom floor frightened like the person everyone thinks I am, curled up in the fetal position, feeling like a loser, a nobody, a someone everyone can forget about. I truly feel, in a world full of colour, I don't belong anywhere except the pitch black, where no-one can see me that way. I can't get in anyone's way except my own. That's what I deserve, nothing. That's why I am nobody worth caring about. **That would be correct, you're a nobody,**

Dylan's Battle

you're a failure, you're doing nothing but using valuable oxygen.

My phone pings, the screen lights up, I lean over, and squint my now sore red eyes because the phone screen is so bright, the face ID doesn't recognize my screwed up face, so I have to enter my password manually, 110720 which is Chloe and I's anniversary. I press the messages app and Chloe's name has got a small blue dot on it. My finger slowly reaches for her text, as my stomach is turning. **You don't deserve her, why even look at the message**. His voice inside my mind is so loud, it's making it difficult to focus, making me forget what I'm supposed to do, **leave her alone, she deserves better than you, why are you even replying to her, she doesn't even love you.**

Dylan's Battle

I close my eyes, take a deep breath in and then count down from ten to re-centre myself.

10.

9.

8.

7.

6.

5.

4.

3.

2.

1.

I open my eyes and go straight to Chloe's text message.

Hey babe, I'm up my nans tonight in Blackwood, I'll give you a ring tonight and I'll be down tomorrow anyway. I love you x

> Morning beautiful, have a lovely time, but no worries I'm not feeling too good today anyway, I have a pounding headache and just want a relaxing day, I love you too x

awh no way? Make sure you rest up, have you been taking your medication, last time you had a bad headache you had stopped taking your anti-depressants?x

Dylan's Battle

> Yeah I'm taking them don't worry, I'm just coming down with a cold or something! I'll text you later, I love you the mostest gorgeous x

Dylan's Battle

Hahaha I've made you resort to lying to the one you love the most, what a shitty fucking boyfriend you are

Chloe and I have always said 'the mostest' since the first time I said I love you, and it's sort of become our little thing. It's something silly but it just shows how much I really do love her. I place my phone back on my bed and go back to the mirror, I realise I'm still in my boxers, not actually getting to the point of putting my jogger on because I'm still extremely aware of his presence.

I mean Chloe is right I haven't been taking my medication. He tells me not to take them all the time. I know I need them, but he keeps telling me that he will hurt Chloe if I do take them. He tells me that I don't even deserve them, that other people deserve them more than I do. He even gets angry when I think about taking them, it's not worth winding him up even more, more shouting, more threats. **That's right you don't deserve them, they are wasted on you when other people want them more.** That's something he always tells me and I guess he is right, what's the point? I won't need them soon anyways so it's not like it matters anymore. **I wish you would just hurry up already. The longer this takes, the harder it's gonna be.**

Dylan's Battle

Chapter Two 10AM Chloe

I stare at my phone thinking about the last couple of texts I've received from Dylan, he has been so distant from me recently I don't really know what's wrong with him. I get in the yellow mini cooper with my mum, she puts on her favourite Taylor Swift album 'reputation'. I remember me and Dylan dancing to this whole album illuminated by the refrigerator light, a few months ago. He seems like a completely different person to the person I first fell in love with. I know Dylan has some sort of past with his mental health. I remember when his nan died he was quiet for months, trying to isolate himself. I've caught him talking and replying to himself a few times as well. Dylan seemed so pissed off but I just couldn't understand what was happening at the time. It

Dylan's Battle

was only later on I thought he must be struggling with his mental health at the moment, I've always known he's been on medication for it, but he never tells me what medication it actually is. The hardest thing for me is when I see his old scars across his arms and thighs where he hurt himself. When I see them, I feel helpless, not being able to help him or guide him. I know he hasn't hurt himself since we've been together, I just wish I got to him earlier, maybe some of those scars wouldn't be there now if I did get there in time.

I genuinely don't know what to do, to help him with whatever is wrong at the moment because he just won't tell me what has been happening over the last couple of months. It's like something has been festering within him, but he just can't tell me what's happening inside his own head.

Dylan's Battle

I put my seatbelt on as my mum reverses out of the driveway. 'Mum what do you do if you can tell that there is something wrong with someone but they just won't tell you what's wrong?' 'Is everything ok Chloe?' Mum looked quite concerned when she said that, I almost felt like I said the wrong thing for a second, before a warm welcoming smile spread across her face. 'Just Dylan mum, he hasn't been himself recently, he said he has been taking his antidepressants but I just don't know how I can tell him, he can talk to me, he can trust me. I just really want to tell him that everything is going to be ok' I can already feel tears trying to escape my eyes as I say this out loud for the first time I feel a little choked up.

Dylan's Battle

I look up at mum's face when that familiar comforting smile spreads across her face 'you gotta remember Chloe, for his age he has been through hell of a lot.'

'He was only 18 when his whole family abandoned him, because his grandmother died and gave him the house. Imagine your whole family deserting you weeks after the person he probably felt closest to him in family passed away, he's going to be feeling lonely and stressed at times, but he always seems to be getting on with it, not letting anything getting in his path, like he has always done, he's a strong boy, he has you.

It's obvious how in love you are with him, you know all of us love Dylan and think of him as one of our own, he's probably just feeling a little lost at the moment, it really does happen to the best of us babe, but everything is going to be fine I promise, just be there for him that is

Dylan's Battle

all you can do, I'm sure that's all he ever wants from you, he loves you to pieces you know that and we know that' 'I know thank you momma'

I stare out the window for the rest of the journey looking back at old photos of me and Dylan, like our first date, we walked around exploring different places in Newport town centre. We watched a busker outside burger king who was actually really good, we watched him sing Bohemian Rhapsody joining in on the mamma mia parts obviously. We had our first kiss in the car park behind Newport leisure centre. I remember how soft his lips were as his hands ran through my hair, or how he became so shy after I laughed because of how awkward I am. He commented on my big puffer jacket and how blonde my hair actually is. I remember feeling his whole

Dylan's Battle

body shaking as I hugged him for the first time, and I remember the small wink he gave me everytime a Tesla drove past because he knew how badly I wanted one. I remember our first concert when we went to see Lady GaGa in Birmingham. Mum drove us all the way up because we weren't old enough to get the coach up on our own yet, to see the 'artrave' concert which everyone used to say that it's her worst album, but we absolutely loved it. We would sing and dance scream DONATELLA all the time, I remember our last concert just before his nan died, we went to see Paramore in Cardiff, we stayed in a hotel that night, and I bought a new lingerie set ready for when we got back to the hotel. I feel a smile start to come across my face, feeling my cheeks turn warm, just thinking about Dylan's reaction to what I was wearing.

Dylan's Battle

That's when everything changed with him though, within 2 months after that his nan died, and it felt like a piece of him died with her. It was after this that he went to the doctors and started taking antidepressants. He didn't have that shine in his eyes anymore, you could see he was getting stressed as he started applying for jobs. You could see something in his head was taking him away from me. I know I can lose my temper with him, it's just because I want to help him so badly but he just won't take it. I truly feel like I'm stuck between a rock and a hard place. The antidepressants tablets he takes has some side effects that seem to be affecting our relationship too. He gets tired so easily, sometimes Dylan says he feels just zombified by them, like they help but his whole body is on autopilot, that all other emotions are just numb, so the tablets work but at the cost of losing other

Dylan's Battle

emotions just to protect his mind. His sex drive is either one of the two extremes, either nothing, or constantly wants to be in bed with me, I don't know if that's catching up, or if it makes him feel wanted and loved if all other emotions are just currently a lost cause. No complaints from me, I just wish he would talk to me about it, so I can help him and make him realise how loved he truly is.

I look out the window and in the distance I can see the metal man, on the roundabout coming up to Blackwood bridge, I imagine how cold he is to touch, what has he witnessed over the years, the heartbreak, the love, the first and last kisses, as he stands tall looking over the bridge, what else will he witness in the years to come?

Dylan's Battle

I have no idea why, but all of a sudden I have just felt knots spreading inside my stomach, something turning my body and blood cold, just like the metal man standing tall, it's making me feel extremely uneasy. I start to well up, tears starting to form, slowly making their way down my face, free falling down creating water marks on my leggings. My mum puts her hand on my leg, and somehow I know everything is going to be ok in the end.

Before I know it my mood is picking up, a smile slowly starts to crawl onto my face as me and mum are singing, track 9 on the 'reputation' album.

As we pull into nans street I look at mum whose eyes are glued on the road ahead, 'thank you for saying that about me and Dylan earlier mum, I really love him, and just get so protective and worried about him' 'I know baby don't worry, it just shows how incredible you actually are with him'

I walk into my nans with a spring in my step, feeling a lot more optimistic than I did 45 minutes ago. Sometimes all you need is a chat with your momma and sing to Taylor Swift's best album to make sure you're doing the right thing.

Dylan's Battle

Chapter Three - Dylan 11am

I'm sitting in a dark corner of my bedroom, I can hear the clock ticking, watching the hours move quicker than ever, the ticking is getting louder and louder. Every tick of the clock feels like a pulse rooted deep inside my brain. I feel like this clock is becoming a part of my brain, I know it's a clock but it feels more like a timer, the timer is escaping my grasp, I can feel the countdown with every breath.

TICK TOCK TICK TOCK TICK TOCK

I close my eyes, rub them hard with my hands in fists and reopen them, I look at the blue wall where the clock was as I slowly realise I have never even had a clock in my bedroom before, yet I can still hear that sound, I can still feel the pulse of the ticking noise. I know I just saw

Dylan's Battle

one right there, with the clock arm spinning faster than an F1 wheel around the track.

My eyes refocus and I'm staring at the shadow that's been following me around, he scares me in ways I have never been scared before, like the pits of my stomach are being pulled out of me, all while a clown is chasing me with my own stomach, it's like being trapped knowing no one can help you from your deepest and scariest fear but you're going to be spending all day dragging around those fears like they are shackled to your ankles dragging them around trying to keep them out of sight, or it's like you're staring at your own dead body. That's how scared I am of the shadow.

Dylan's Battle

You should be scared of me because no one is coming to help you HAHAHA you're going to die scared just like you fucking deserve, do you really think anyone cares enough to help you or care enough about you, you are truly fucked Dylan.

'STOP FUCKING TALKING TO ME, LEAVE ME ALONE PLEASE' **IT'S TIME YOU END ALL OF THIS DYLAN ITS TIME TO FUCKING DIE.**

I close my eyes weeping, I get my AirPods, and take the AirPods out of the case, and slowly insert them into my ears, double checking first they are going into the correct ear.

With my Airpods in, I unlock my phone, and go to my safety net, the music app; The best 7.99 I spend a month on. I click artists and press Christina Perri, I go to her 'head or heart' album, I then go straight to track 4. I concentrate on the music, with my eyes closed, the chords of the piano feeling like they are going slower than my own heart beat, the individual instruments, the pure raw vocal and every breath I hear her take and I concentrate on the lyrics.

'But I'm only human

And I bleed when I fall down

I'm only human

And I crash and I break down **I WISH YOU WOULD, DIE DIE DIE DIE**

Your words in my head, knives in my heart

The knives are in the kitchen. Why don't you get them? You know the next door neighbours are

Dylan's Battle

talking about you right now? Probably about to ring the police on you, for being such a piece of shit
You build me up and then I fall apart
'Cause I'm only human"

I open my eyes slowly, dreading what I'll see when I fully open them. As my eyes adjust to the lighting of the room, I see him, he is standing right in front of me, with this daunting smile that I know is only trouble. I throw my phone at him, even though I know it's going to go straight through him, I know he isn't there, I know I am the only person who can see him, I know there is no one else having this torture put on them every single day, yet he is so real to me, I can hear his voice, sometimes multiple voices telling me to die, to hurt myself and to end my own life, even though it isn't his life to take; but still his after all the horrible evil manipulative things he says to me his mouth never moves when he talks.

I can smell his aftershave almost like this earthy, sour scent that gets stuck so far up my nose it makes me want to throw up whatever is inside my stomach, I can see what he looks like.

A tall Chinese man, he wears a green chequered shirt, a long black neatly done tie, fitted black trousers and smart shoes, he's wearing three bright glistening medals on the left side of his chest, he has short black hair, cobbled to the left of his head, he has the brightest yet most crooked teeth I've ever seen, his breath always smells like some form of acid that is definitely not pleasant. He is holding an object in his hand, even though I have never seen what it is, I always assume it's a piece of paper, but it's

Dylan's Battle

always so blurry I really couldn't say for sure what exactly it is.

I go and sit on my double bed and find Chloe's thong from a couple of days ago, I usually feel dead and numb inside, feeling nothing but the nothingness and emptiness running thru my veins, feeling so cold and dead but the feeling of Chloe makes me feel something, the pleasure, the love, the tenderness, the height of both of our orgasms. Even though he is always watching me, Chloe doesn't need to know that, his eyes always watching, him always shouting **she will probably fuck someone else after you, because we all know you can't do the job, your a dip it in and done kind of guy, she needs someone who can satisfy her.**

Dylan's Battle

I always try to ignore him, because she seems to enjoy it, but I truly don't think people know how hard it is to try and concentrate to make sure Chloe feels safe and comfortable, when I don't feel any of those things either.

I close my eyes and try and take my mind back there, feeling her mouth travelling down my neck, her hands rubbing against my bulge as my hands explore her, the small gasps of breaths she takes as I slowly insert my fingers inside of her, the feeling of how tight she is wrapped around my fingers, or the feeling of the warmth of her hand as she wraps it around my hardened dick. I move my own hand with my eyes still closed pretending I'm Chloe, rubbing my semi-hardened dick.
As I stroke it becoming hard, I remember the way Chloe moans as I slowly take off her panties, making sure my

Dylan's Battle

knuckles brush against her as I slowly take them down, Remembering the way Chloe tastes, while her legs are wrapped tight around my neck, and her hands pushing my head down even deeper.

 I remember he nails digging into my back as I slowly insert myself inside of her, with her starting to moan and beg as we both thrust as one and both slowly edge to a climax. Remembering the way she would bite my lip as she would pull me into her, kissing her while almost going deeper inside of her, feeling her toes curl, the louder she got, trying to arch her back, so I could go that little bit deeper, her quirky laugh if it ever slipped out during sex, knowing I was going to push it back in so hard, I was almost guaranteed a good moan out of it. Thinking back I'm sure she does it on purpose. Her hands are always above her head, while I hold them down, knowing I'm going to be sinking deep inside of her, ready to finish, I'd almost always thrust as deep as I could while I kiss her lips, and slowly bite her bottom lip as I pull away from her.

I slowly feel myself climbing to a climax, about to feel a small amount of euphoria, or a small amount of anything to be honest.

DO YOU REALLY THINK YOU DESERVE THESE FEELINGS, you don't deserve to feel anything, let alone anything with Chloe, leave your dick alone, you need to spend time with ME. Be careful I know people are watching you while you play with your silly little dick, they are probably recording you this very second. Put it all over your

Dylan's Battle

social media, wait until thousands of people have watched you, laughing at you, your family hating you even more, Chloe leaving you. What's even the point anymore?

You see this is how it always is, he never leaves me, whatever I do, whatever I try, he is constantly there, trying to take away any feeling I try and gain, a small glimpse of almost happiness and he has to also take that away from me, sucking any emotions out of me, no matter what I do, no matter where I am, he is always watching me, shouting at me, swearing at me, ready to pounce, the first chance he gets, and do you know what? It is fucking exhausting, I don't know how much more of this I can take, my head is filled with so many voices that I can't even count all the different things that are being thrown around inside my mind..

Die.

Are the neighbours still talking about you?

I wonder if Chloe is cheating on your right now?

I bet your nan is glad she is dead just to get the fuck away from you.

Why don't you join your nan and ask her

No wonder why your whole family abandoned you, do you really think you deserve all this

I hide under my duvet quivering, crying and screaming' leave me alone please, leave me alone' why am I the person who sees him, hears him. Why is it me who has to live this stupid fucking life.

Dylan's Battle

I am so angry.

I feel so alone.

I feel so empty.

I feel defeated.

You know what you have to do Dylan. It's time to finish this now, it's time, you give up, you know you need to leave everything behind, and give everything you have to someone who actually deserves it, what are you doing wasting Chloe's time, you know she's just going to move on, you may as well finish it and leave now. Leave your relationship, she's cheating on you anyway, someone told me.

I stand up, wipe my face with my arm and finally get dressed.

Dylan's Battle

Unknown Figure

The more I upset and scare Dylan, the stronger I become. I get an even better grasp of him, he will finally do what he has to do. He's already breaking, you can see him crumbling, like a dialect building slowly crumbling from the bottom slowly engulfing the whole building as it falls to the ground.

This is one battle I will win, Dylan is mine if he likes it or not.

Dylan's Battle

Chapter Four - Dylan 12PM

I slowly walk down the stairs, aware of every wooden floor board under my feet, every step feeling heavier than the other, still wondering how the fuck I fell into this situation, this isn't the person I was suppose to become. **This is always the person you were supposed to be a loser, a nobody, make sure you check that the front door is locked, remember the neighbours are trying to kill you.**

I run to the front door, totally forgetting the heaviness in my feet, double checking and triple checking that the front door is one hundred percent locked. I run into the kitchen and make sure all the knife's are where they are supposed to be, I check the back door, and then run and check the front door again just in case. **They are coming to get you, you're dead meat.**

I run and check the curtains and make sure the windows are shut, I double check to see that the neighbours are not home at the minute so that's calming me down.

They've gone out to buy the murder weapons, what are you going to do now? Your time is almost up, Dylan you're about to die.

I feel my heart racing and panic setting in.

My breaths are getting quicker and shallower, I feel faint, I'm so exhausted. Sweat pours from my forehead, dripping into my eyes, mixing with my tears.

My hands are uncontrollable with how much they're shaking. My mouth is unbearably dry, not being able to swallow, feeling like I have sand filling every gap inside my throat. The room is spinning just as fast as the clock was in my bedroom, unable to get my bearings, he is the only thing that remains standing still in this dizzying haze. He's staring at me, he's laughing at me, he's taunting me. **You're having a heart attack now you really are going to die.** I try to clutch my t-shirt, feeling the pain in my chest. I go to sit on the brown leather sofa that nan loved when she was still here. My head feels like it doesn't even belong to me, like I've lost all sense of what's happening at this very moment. **You can't even say goodbye, this is your final breath Dylan.** I close my eyes accepting my final breath.

Dylan's Battle

I must wake up not 5 minutes later realising I must have fainted from having a panic attack, not a heart attack. The room slows down and then stops spinning, my hands are slightly more steady, my mouth is still so dry that I must have swallowed a building's worth of saw dust, but it wasn't a heart attack, I'm ok.

You can't even die properly what is even the fucking point?

I stand up, re-adjusting, I recheck all the doors and windows, making sure I am still safe. I pick my phone up, unlock it and go to Uber eats, realising I should probably eat if I've just passed out.

I go straight to McDonald's. I order my usual, which is a large Big Mac meal with no pickles and a Diet Coke with no ice. If Chloe was here she would have 9 chicken nuggets, with a large fries and a large coke with no ice. I

Dylan's Battle

put my order into my basket and it comes to £9.92. I hit the order button and it says a half hour to 45 minutes delivery wait time, which is no issue. I've been telling myself for some time now that I should get started on designing my first tattoo, so this gives me some time to actually sit down. I've been trying to design this tattoo for months but as you can imagine, I tend to get distracted. My head never seems to be able to concentrate long enough for me to finish a task.

I go and grab my AirPods, I chuck them in my ear, open up my music app, go to my playlists and hit 'favourite songs ever' playlist. It's a playlist me and Chloe made one night after we had a stupid argument about how Chloe got angry at me because I didn't want to visit her island on 'Animal Crossing: New Horizons. Looking back at that argument now it was pretty funny, seeing her lip quiver she was genuinely that upset I didn't want to see her talking animals on her Pushpea island, I'd do anything to be sat on the bed with her at that moment, disappearing into a false sense of reality creating my own piece of paradise hiding away from the horror that is real life. **You're already wishing to get away from the life you have now, this is going to be so easy to get rid of you, just like wiping shit off my shoe.**

In my ears I hear the familiar tune and voice of 'Lady GaGa which always makes the corner of my lips rise ever so slightly

'I am so fab

Check out, I'm blonde, I'm skinny, I'm rich

And I'm a little bit of a bitch'

Dylan's Battle

This song always reminds me of Chloe and I screaming this song at the top of our voices pretending we are the best singers ever to exist on this planet, I can picture her now, in her favourite cream cardigan, with three stars climbing up the sleeve, her hair falling down her back, eyes closed lost in the moment, she looked at peace, lost within her own small world, singing and dancing like she is creating a core memory in this very moment with me. **That will never be you, wait did I hear a car park up, this is it, they're coming to kill you.**

I run to the window almost feeling like everything is in slow motion, I watched my Airpod slowly fall, landing onto the floor, before bouncing three times before settling down onto the floor, I slowly pull back the

Dylan's Battle

curtain, just enough that my eyes are visible, no car there, I am safe for a small amount of time, before they really do come and kill me. Should I arm myself ready for when they do come and kill me? **What's the point, your dead already Dylan, why prolong the inevitable?**

Now I know I'm not facing immediate danger, **you are** I follow my previous steps, and pick up my Airpod that fell onto the floor I slowly put it back into my ear,I hear a raspy voice singing the words

'Unbreak the broken,
Unsay these spoken words,
 Find hope in the hopeless,
 Pull me out of the train wreck'

Dylan's Battle

I chuckle out of how fucking ironic that is, because let's be honest, this is an absolute shit show I'm in, I don't even know if there is a way out of this train wreck, and if there is I either need an epiphany too show me how this works, or I need at least thirteen miracles.

You need more than that, you're on your own kid, you're stuck just me and you, forever, unless you can think of a way to get rid of me, but lets be honest we both know you're fucked in the head, it will always just be me and you.

I feel myself getting angrier and angrier with him, I just don't know how to shut him up, to turn him off, to make him leave my head. He's been here for just over six months now? The words he spits with such venom getting worse every single day, I know he means every word he says I know how much he wants me gone, away

Dylan's Battle

from this life time, I don't know how much more I can take, but I also know, surely he can't say much worse than what he is already telling me, pretty consistently now, but I'm almost starting to believe that maybe he is right.

I walk over to the dining room table, where my notebook and pencils are, to the left is a normal pencil and to the right is a week old cup of coffee, I'm only guessing it's about a week old from the mould floating on top of the stone cold milky liquid. I try to focus and draw this fucking tattoo I've been wanting for years now, after falling in love with the song but I have never been able to visualise how I'd want this tattoo to look until now which is strange really, while my head is tormenting me more than ever, I'm able to put to paper what I've been

Dylan's Battle

trying to create inside my own mind, even in the darkest of moments, I am now able to visual this tattoo perfectly. I pick up my pencil and slowly feel my wrist creating cursive patterns and loops, before I know it, I've created this beautiful rose, all the loops are how my brain is currently feeling, dizzying, confusion, scared, lonely, yet I am still able to create something beautiful with all these scared and *probably* paranoid feelings I'm having, but that's just part of who I am at the moment, and there isn't a lot going on at the moment other than that, I mean I am only human right?

I connect the lines flowing from the rose, and place my pencil down and for at least this very second while I stare at this piece of art I've just created I feel a sense of peace run through my veins through my body, starting at my toes, slowly circulating itself up my legs. I feel the weight being lifted from my stomach, releasing from the pain that has been holding everything down. The sense of peace carries on spreading towards my heart, when it finally hits my brain, I get this rush of quietness and serenity within my mind.

Dylan's Battle

I close my eyes, take a long peaceful breath and just for a millisecond I feel like everything is okay.

The next millisecond is a different feeling altogether, my heart starts to pump, I can feel my heart beating faster and faster like it's about to burst through my chest cavity and all I'm going to be is a dead body on the floor, better than the neighbours killing me though right? I start to feel the sweat pouring down my face, the clammy feeling in my hands, the panic has well and truly set in; before I know it, it's got really loud here, is it inside the house? Or is it just my mind tormenting me again, I can hear 100s of different voices, getting louder and louder, all screaming different things.

Dylan's Battle

DIE   KILL YOURSELF RUN QUICK CHLOE DOESNT LOVE YOU. SHES PROBABLY CHEATING ON YOU, NO ONE EVER LOVED YOU

YOURE GOING TO DIE ALONE

THAT KNIFE IS OVER THERE LETS STOP THIS FUUUCCCCKKKK YOU   OH SHIT THE NEIGHBOURS ARE HOME   WHY DONT YOU FUCKING STOP WASTING ALL THIS OXYGEN.

I can see him laughing at me, he's standing in the corner; he's laughing yet I can't hear any of that. I squeeze my eyes closed as hard as I can, I take my Airpods out and put my hands over my ears, how does he have so many voices that are just getting louder. I feel this gut wrenching feeling inside my belly, I feel tears flowing down my cheeks. This is fucking exhausting.

AHHHH FUCKING DIE   WHY DONT YOU JUST FUCKING END THIS YOURE NOTHING DYLAN FUCK YOU   ITS TIME TO END THIS. AHHHHH, FUCK YOU, YOURE GOING TO DIE, FUCKING SCREAM, NO ONE IS HERE TO FUCKING HELP YOU.   YOU'RE GOING TO DIE ALL ALONE AND NO ONE CAN OR WILL LOVE YOU. DIE DIE DIE DIE DIE DIE DIE FUCK YOU DIE DIE DIE KILL YOUR FUCKING SELF DIE DIE DIE DIE DIE DIE DIE DIE ARGHHHHHH DIE DIE DIE DYLAN YOU'RE FUCKING WORTHLESS

Dylan's Battle

EVERYONE LEFT YOU FOR A FUCKING REASON DYLAN YOU'RE NOTHING.

DIE

LEAVE ME ALONE LEAVE ME ALONE AHH, please just leave me alone, what have I done to deserve this?

Die die die

A scream rips out of my throat, it feels sore, red raw, like I've just swallowed fifty razorblades down in one. Just as I start to taste blood, I hear a knock on the door, **This is it, the neighbours are coming to kill you Dylan this is it, you're dead meat.**

Dylan's Battle

I'm screaming, the sides of my throat collapsing from within, becoming nothing but chunks of flesh, dissolving with every desperate cry for help I create. The soreness and pain of standing on a piece of Lego, then forcing it down my throat. 'FUCK OFF, LEAVE ME BE, I DONT DESERVE THIS'

Through the postbox, a gentleman shouts, 'McDonald's delivery', I slowly tiptoe to the front door, hearing a creak in the floor boards. I take a brief look through the stained glass window in our front door and can see a blurry orange bag.

I slowly unlock the door and take this man in, he is about 5 ft and 3 stone soaking wet.

I give a small smile as I slowly open the door a bit more.
I apologised to him, saying I was singing a song, I tried to explain that I clearly listen to heavy metal music.

Dylan's Battle

I lied.

I thank him, and slowly go to the table, I place the paper bag on the table, and take my order out.

Fucking choke dylan

I close my eyes, take a deep breath in, I can smell the food, clinging to me and as I eat my food with each bite more cautious than the last, I feel like I'm slowly drowning, barely grasping enough oxygen for the next breath, the next bite, the next struggle.

Dylan's Battle

Chapter Five - Chloe 1pm

I'm sitting on my nan's sofa, while mum and nan are gossiping in the kitchen. Nan must have recently cleaned the sofa cushions, the smell of the fabric conditioner is intoxicating my sense of smell, slowly climbing up my nose bringing memories to the fore-front of my brain of my grandad, who passed away a couple of years ago from kidney failure. Grandad and I always used to have pillow fights on the sofa or we would be watching some cooking tutorial on youtube, while shouting instructions at nan telling her what to cook next, always telling her not to over cook the rice. I look over the left of the telly and see a photo of me and Dylan from when we went to prom, which feels like a lifetime ago now, I walk over and pick up the photo stuck in my own little world, when life was so much simpler, easier, when the love was so strong and raw.

 He knocked on my front door, all nervous wearing a full 3 piece suit with a pink dickie bow, I remember him being a little too adamant about wanting the dickie bow. I argued that maybe he should wear a tie, but he said the dickie bow would suit his eyes. We laughed for hours, until the side of our stomach was aching. Even a few teachers were laughing, knowing Dylan always had to be different. Miss Glynne seemed to appreciate the dickie bow though. I almost got jealous for a second, before remembering she was a teacher, and Dylan was all mine, and we would stand the test of time. Just Dylan, me and that fucking dickie bow.

Dylan's Battle

I remember the look in his eyes when he saw me in my prom dress for the first time. They glowed and his mouth dropped. He tried to hug me, but the purple prom dress was too puffy, almost like the shape of candy floss on a stick, he laughed and looked embarrassed. He handed me a bouquet of flowers, he complimented me and my dress. My dress oh my god it was gorgeous, a BITCH to put on though. Dylan didn't seem to struggle taking it off though, the first time for the both of us, a magical night that I'll cherish forever.

The feeling of Dylan's lips pressed against mine, as we watched the firework display, a thousand different fireworks going off inside my stomach in sync with the colourful glow illuminating the sky above us. The sparks that came off our lips while they were connected, felt even brighter than the ones in the sky. I felt this new type of warmth spread through my entire body as our lips slowly separated knowing we needed to be connected in an even deeper meaning.

'Chloe would you like a cup of tea?' I heard my nan shout in the distance bringing me back into the real world.

'Yes please nan, 1 sugar milk please' I called back before going back into my daydream that I desperately needed.

I pull out my phone, go back to my photos, and find a selfie of when we went to watch 'A Star is Born' on some cricket pitch in Cardiff, I started recording Dylan towards the end knowing he had never seen the film before. I remember his shoulders shifting mountains as he sobbed from his own breaking heart while the film's final scenes rolled out.

I swipe right, there is a photo of Dylan and I, our smiles spreading across Bristol harbour, all the restaurants and pubs behind us. We walked for hours hand in hand putting the world to right, exploring a new city where no-one knew us. A place where we could be truly whoever we wanted to be. We laughed hearing someone murdering a song on karaoke. We danced along to all the different music playing from separate buildings throughout the main street.

'CHLOE' nan shouted with some sort of annoyance in her voice.

'Sorry nan, I must of been of daydreaming again'

Dylan's Battle

'You bloody lot and your phones got a lot to answer for that apple thing, drink up because we will be going into Blackwood and Asda to get some treats ready for film night, what are we fancy watching? I know that A Star is Born is on catch up, you know how I feel about that Bradley Cooper'

Chloe felt a smile start to ascend across her face and in that moment she knew from this very moment everything was okay.

'Sounds like the perfect night nan'

I open up my phone and text Dylan to tease him about what I'm watching tonight. I can't wait to give him the biggest hug and kiss tomorrow.

hey baby, how's your headache? Make sure you're drinking enough water please 🙏 you'll never guess what me and Nan are watching tonight, A Star Is Born!! What a date night that was 😉 I love you the mostest babe, can't wait for cuddles and kisses tomorrow x

Dylan's Battle

Dylan texts back within the minute, telling me he is having a McDonalds. He felt weird not ordering 9 nuggets for me but liked how much cheaper it was without my order, with laughing faces obviously.

Dylan is always trying to make sure he seems okay even if he isn't. Tomorrow I'll be there to double check everything with him though, it will all be okay. The universe has given me that confirmation with the film we are watching, all the films in the whole world that nan could have chosen, she picked 'A Star Is Born'. I text Dylan back one more time to remind him that I truly love him the mostest and then kiss the screen where his face appears on my home screen.

I finish my cup of tea, walk into the kitchen to place it on the side. I give mum the biggest hug, knowing everything will be okay. I take a deep breath to recenter myself and then step out the front door with everyone together to go to Asda.

Dylan's Battle

Chapter Six - Dylan 2pm

I finish up my food, place it into the recycling and grab my phone, Airpods and put my shoes on. I really need to get out of this fucking house. **You really think you can fucking walk away from me, it's really that easy huh? Don't you remember your fucking neighbours are coming to kill you**

'YOUR NOT FUCKING REAL, THEY ARE NOT GOING TOO FUCKING KILL ME, YOU ARE'

I slam my front door, locking it behind me. Slowly walking down the street, I admire the space around me, the cloudy skies, the cars parked up around me, the green bin in the middle of the street, and the 'special flat' at the top of the road, which we all know is a drug den, but no one ever mentions that out loud. I cross the road, turn left heading straight towards George street bridge.

Dylan's Battle

I grab my phone out of my pocket and start playing my favourite playlist. My eyes gaze across the view as I hit the peak of the bridge, stopping to look over and seeing another 2 bridges ahead of me. The one bridge, everyone calls the walking bridge because you can only walk over it. You can see its 2 massive white metal poles pointing in almost arrows, where the metal base is at the bottom for you to walk over it, and then in the far distance you see a red bridge which is just in front of a small castle. My nan used to call that the 'moshers' castle. I have no idea why, but there we go, as I head towards the end of the bridge I notice bumpy bits on the pavement, I'm cautious to avoid the bumps so I'm not tripping over them. While my eyes are focused on the unsteady pavement, I read the graffiti on the cold concrete floor. I take a step back. I feel a thud in my stomach.

I close my eyes, the earth feels like it's doing an extra rotation, the world spinning faster than ever before. I re-open my eyes and it's still there 'dylan die' they can't mean me surely? I close my eyes again and focus on the music.

I reopen them, and my eye's re-adjust to the light around me, the graffiti is gone.

HAHAHAHA.

I carry on walking, butI hear him laughing at me. He always seems to be at least 10 steps ahead of me, he knows what I'm doing, he knows where I'm going even before I get there. I just need five minutes of nothing in my head, I just need that time, because this is

Dylan's Battle

exhausting, just five minutes is all I'm really asking for, is that too much to really ask for?

I keep on walking to the beat of my music, past the hospital, where the worst memories have happened. I lost nan in that hospital. I sat next to her, I held her hand. She wasn't conscious, I looked over to her, and saw all the years she had lived scattered around her face, burrowed deep into the wrinkles. I saw her fingers, but I also saw all of the things they had touched, all of the things she felt in her lifetime. Everything she created with those hands, her famous curry sauce where she would never tell us her recipe, or all the woolly hats she made for people, through different stages of our lives. I remember telling her I love her, and that it's time to go. Go back to grandad, we will see eachother again one day, but for now I'll be ok, you need to rest, I love you. I kissed her cheek then I just sat there. I felt my shoulders shake, and tears fall onto my t-shirt like a blood stain that will never be removed, nan left us and finally reunited with grandad.

I never actually met my grandad but I know how much nan loved him, and now I'm happy they are finally together again.

Walking past the hospital I realise I'm not ok, I know I'm really struggling, I need nans advice, she would know how to beat this, how to tackle this, but everything happens for a reason right? Of course I'll be ok.

You think you'll be ok, the only time you'll be ok, is when you're in a fucking box.

Dylan's Battle

I ignore him, focusing on the music, zoning in on the singer's voice, to drown everything else out, I turn the music up as loud as it can become. I close my eyes, and slow my breathing down, the world has almost stopped moving, my heart rate has slowed down, I feel a lightness in my head, I feel a lightness in my heart, at last pure serenity. I hold onto this feeling, this moment for as long as possible, not taking a second of this feeling for granted. I feel like the floor is air, swirling and dancing around my feet, every time I place one foot in front of the other it's a cloud that is helping my foot down to the softness off the floor. I make my way past big Tescos, and to my left I see a row of shops. I actually think I felt a smile creep over my face, when I looked at someone walking past. What I'm feeling now is the feeling of hope. I can do this.

Dylan's Battle

At this moment I know nan, is standing by me, holding my hand, fighting the demon away from me, just so I can have my five minutes of serenity.

Thank you nanny.

I turn my music off on my phone, and the silence remains in my head. For the first time today, I am truly at peace with my mind. Absorbing the scenery as I walk closer to Tredegar Park. I stand and stare as cars go off the roundabout, some fast, some slow. They're all heading in different directions with their own separate lives. I stand and wonder where they are going next.

I carry on with my walk.

I reach the bus stop where there is a bench, it's far to small for anyone to fucking sit on unless you're a 3 year old but still able to place atleast a quarter of a butt cheek on it.

Dylan's Battle

All of a sudden the pit of my stomach feels like it's being attacked, it feels like it's doing a thousand rotations, with a knife. I stand up from the incredibly small bench, close my eyes, take deep breaths, slow my breathing down, fuck, nothings happening. The cars start going faster and faster, all of a sudden I realise I'm dripping from the rain, soaked right through. I can feel the squelch in my shoes as I'm standing there, my hair is drenched and I hadn't even noticed I thought it was a nice sunny day. I don't know what's controlling my legs but I feel myself walking closer to the road, the cars seem to be getting faster and faster, my stomach churning, I feel that pit inside of my belly, struggling to contain itself about to burst and explode.

FUCKING

JUMP

Dylan's Battle

Chapter Seven - Dylan 3pm

The ground is spinning around faster than it should be going, doing laps around the solar system, doing laps around my head, at speeds not even recognizable. The serenity in my mind has disappeared, I feel a shooting sensation in my ankle, spearing through my entire body. He put me into this sense false of security and then scared the fucking shit into me, bringing everything back down to reality. I can hear him laughing, pointing at my ankle, laughing louder and louder.

HAHAHAHAHAHAHAHAHAHAHAHA

I must of fallen, when he shouted, tripped on my own beliefs everything was going to okay I suppose, how fucking ironic. At Least most of the people of Newport don't really like human interaction, so I'm pretty sure no-one is going to be coming over to me.

Dylan's Battle

I look at my ankle, the swelling is almost immediate. I touch the most painful area, going just around it, subconsciously checking all the bones are all still where they are supposed to be. I check my pockets for my phone, but there is just an empty space in my pocket. I look around while I'm still flat on my arse, I see my phone to my left, must have skidded across the floor. While I was falling back into reality, falling back into the darkest place I know, my own battle in my own head. I reach over and grab my naked phone, because apparently I'm one of those cocky people who think they don't need a phone case. I pick it up, and slowly turn it over, like I'm on the show 'deal or no deal' slowly opening my red box. The screen is shattered, just like my mind.

Dylan's Battle

You can't even look after your phone, and keep that safe when I'm around, so how do you think you're going to keep yourself safe.

Dylan you're next.

FUCK you, I scream it letting everything out. He fucking gave me hope, but he just took it away as quickly, playing god with my own life how is that fair? He knew and deep down I suppose I know I'm never going to feel like that again.

I place my hands, on the hard cold, wet floor, and slowly lift myself up, with my good ankle, slowly putting pressure on the probably twisted ankle, a sharp hot pain, scolding up my leg.

Dylan's Battle

I let out a welp like a wounded animal as I walk two steps, each step burning hotter with every bit of pressure applied. I'm visibly limping through gritted teeth.

Give up, it's not worth it, just sit there, you don't deserve all this determination. You think your phone is fucking shattered, you wait until I'm finished with you. I'm a volcano, and I'm bubbling over, your the lava, about to tip over the fucking edge. You and I Dylan, we are about to erupt if you like it or not.

I stagger slowly the way I came, taking regular breaks, the walk now feeling like a real bad idea. My ankle is becoming more and more noticeable swelling up and piercing throughout my body. I feel the burning through my ankle travelling into my stomach, making me feel physically sick. I walk past the hospital ignoring all signs mentally and physically telling me to go in there, GET HELP.

This is your last chance to get rid of me Dylan.

It's a trap, he'll never fucking leave just get home, home is safe, home is a comfort zone where I can let out all my grievances.

I have one journey I'm worried about, I know he is going to shout at me, that voice no one else can hear. I'm nearing the bridge, and do you know what? I'm really fucking scared.

Are you strong enough to get over the bridge Dylan, maybe the only thing you can do is climb over that barrier. Maybe the only thing you can do is jump off. Do you know how to get rid of me? FUCKING JUMP DO US ALL A FAVOUR YOU'RE FUCKED.

Dylan's Battle

I'm right behind you, I'm going to push you, I'm going to hurt you, I'm going to kill you.

Dylan's Battle

Chapter Eight - Dylan 3:40pm

My feet are cemented to the floor, unsure if I'm going to be able to lift them from the ground. **IT WOULD BE BETTER IF YOU GOT TO THE MIDDLE OF THE BRIDGE AND JUMPED IT WILL BE BETTER TO WATCH**

I'm frozen in time, not sure how to listen to these threats, self-doubt, flooding into my veins, not sure why i'm on this planet, to live in torture? To live a struggle? To suffer more or less alone. **Exactly no one is going to miss you, only your pretty little girl, but she will find someone better, she deserves better than you, it's time you let her go. Climb the barrier Dylan. DO IT.** I grab my headphones and inhale what feels like most of the oxygen in Newport. I unlock my phone slicing the tip of my finger in the process, fucking thing. **You think your**

Dylan's Battle

headphones solve everything, DO NOT piss me off Dylan, this doesn't end well for you.

Someone walking past, touches my shoulder, their hand feeling so much warmer compared to the hoody now sticking to my skin from it being drenched with this rain. 'Hi, are you okay? You look freezing, I saw you limping, as you were walking?' I look up, and turn towards them, their grey wispy hair, looking so much like nan, their hands looking frail, but they have such a reassuring smile. I tell her that I'm ok, and told her how I tripped over a branch **fucking liar** 'thank you so much for asking, it has just been a pretty rough day, the weather certainly does'nt help either. The lady gave me a warm smile and went on her way.

My feet have now started the motion of putting one foot in front of the other, I focus on the beat, I focus again on

Dylan's Battle

Christina Perri's voice. I listen as the chorus builds, I'm only human. I look to my left and see those two bridges again, it feels like the earth has done a thousand laps since I last saw them. My hands touch the cold rusty bar of the barrier, **do it, climb over, jump, you only deserve to die.** I hold my breath, I weigh up my options. Maybe it would be easier if I just do what he says? I place one foot on the metal bar, giving my bad ankle a break from the weight. I look down and see the murky river water. I try to imagine how it would feel, my body making an impact with the water, would I already be dead by the time I hit the water? Do I die as I make impact, or do I drown filling my lungs with the dirty water that snakes around Newport and surrounding areas.

I step down from the barrier, I'm not going to let him win.

DO IT **DO IT**

DO IT

DO IT   **DO IT**

FUCKING DO IT

DYLAN

WELL WHY DON'T YOU JUST LEAVE ME ALONE, WHAT WILL IT TAKE FOR YOU TO JUST LEAVE ME ALONE. I sob trying to get those words out and trying to catch my breath at the same time. It almost feels like the water really is filling up my lungs.

Dylan's Battle

You know what you have to do Dylan, we can make this right, we can end all of this together now. I'm here to help you.

This can't be the only answer, but I really don't see or feel another way out. I lower my body down and sit on the floor, I place my ankle out, making sure not to put it in an even more painful position. My hair is soaked, my clothes are dripping, my energy levels are lower than ever, and I feel like I need to go back to basics and try again. I just want to curl up into the foetal position and hit restart. I turn the volume up on my phone to maximum. **You won't last long Dylan,** This isn't over Dylan, I won't stop until you're dead. Good luck with the rest of your day, you won't see midnight. Fuck you

His voice slowly fading until there is nothing left, I feel the tears tipping over, falling down further and further into the abyss. If I don't get myself home, I'm worried he is going to beat me. I stand up, apply a small amount of pressure to the ankle that feels like it's going to buckle any moment now, and with every agonising step, I take my time.

I slowly make my way back to my safe place.

Home.

Dylan's Battle

Chapter Nine - Dylan 5pm

I unlock the door, and can feel everything in my body shivering, it feels like an internal body earthquake. I place my hand on the handle, the cold metal handle carving its shape into my hand, I step inside, and the smell of old McDonalds hit's my nostrils. I lock the front door, lean against it and chuckle to myself, that poor delivery guy, maybe I should have given him a tip after hearing my small melt down. I can't believe I said I was singing, that's one angry fucking song. **Believing your own lies now, are you Dylan?** Oh why don't you just fuck off, I don't need you right now, I was having a moment. **One of your last Dylan.** I run my hands through my hair, in disbelief that this is my life, how did I end up here. I stand up kicking off my soaking wet trainers, and slowly walk up the stairs.

Dylan's Battle

I count the stairs one by one, I feel the wooden floor boards, my wet ridden socks leaving imprints on the old creaky stairs. My ankle is still throbbing, but definitely only a sprain. **You might want to cut it off, what if it is infected, what if it kills you, before I do HAHAHAHAHAHAHA** I climb the last of the stairs and go into my doorway for my bedroom. I look around the bedroom and observe everything that is in here. To my left is my mirror, then my chest of draws, with pictures of me and Chloe on, from various dates. One photo from our first date we went to cineworld and Frankie and Bennies restaurant. We took the selfie just after we had our first kiss on a random bridge just before she was walking the rest of the way home, her lips tingling on mine, the butterflies swarming around my belly and I truly felt weak to my knees, and every kiss has felt like that since. **She's probably kissing someone else right now, because even she knows you're a piece of shit**. I look at my side table, all the empty mugs, the dirty plates, the posters on the wall, I see the poster of my favourite album, it's the album artwork to Christina Perri - Head or Heart. My other posters, slowly falling down, the thought of sorting everything out, is so overwhelming I feel like anything else to happen is just going to tip me over the edge. I see him standing there once again, smiling. I hear him coming closer to me. **Boo**, he says in such a whisper, that it actually pisses me off, I can feel fire in my stomach, I can feel my adrenaline hitting me in the veins, I can sense anger climbing my body, clinging onto every single inch of me. WHY DONT YOU JUST FUCK OFF, I see red, my ankle no longer hurting me whatsoever, I run into my room, push my mirror onto the floor, hearing it smash, broken pieces of mirror scattered across the floor, my throat becoming red raw while I scream as I swipe pictures of me and Chloe, now flying across the room. The frames breaking, the glass cracking, the photos ruined, I pick up a mug and throw it at the man no one else can see, it smashes into pieces as it makes contact with the wall, completely going through him. He disappears to another part of the room. **Nice try Dylan, is that all you got?** My anger heightens past my height as I launch another two mugs, and three plates at him, crockery flying like bullets in all directions in my room. I grab my posters, rip them off my walls, falling to the ground a lot more gracefully than I'm currently being. IS THIS WHAT YOU FUCKING WANT HUH WELL COME AND FUCKING GET IT.

Dylan's Battle

I always knew you was fucking weak, how easy was that, to make you snap.

FUCK YOU, I go to my chest of draws and rip the draws out, clothes flying everywhere, the wooden draw crashing onto the floor, the side falling off with a crash when it makes contact with the floor, then I notice a white envelope that has circled the room, and then everything went quiet is was just me and this envelope. No him. Just me and this envelope.

My eyes stayed centred on the envelope, I haven't seen that since nan gave it to me, in hospital the day she was told she had 48 hours left, deep down she must have known she didn't have long left, hence the letter, I've never felt like I could read it, maybe today is the day I can read her last words to me, as the envelope is pulling me closer to the final goodbye.

Dylan's Battle

I feel my eyelids close as I recenter myself, this is what he wants. Why am I letting him just completely ruin me? I take a deep breath in, I can see him in the corner looking around laughing at me. I can see him clapping his hands, like I've just given him a performance of a lifetime. I look around my room, and find myself in the middle of a warzone, everything on the floor, smashed ceramic dishes everywhere, my photos and posters ruined. I'm still standing in soaking wet clothes, they feel heavier and heavier. They feel like they are stuck to my skin with super glue. I pick up my mirror which is shattered into small pieces, the mirror remains whole but broken, with only a few shards on the floor. I stare at my shattered, broken reflection, I take off my clothes, starting with my hoodie, T-shirt, then jeans, boxers and socks. I stare at my naked body and bare skin.

Dylan's Battle

I see old scars across my legs, on my thighs, across my arms, I look down in shame knowing the collection is about to grow. I pick up the envelope, and turn it over, there it is her beautiful hand writing, with the words 'to my one and only Dylan' I almost feel my eyes swelling but nothing fell. I pick up a sharp piece of broken mirror, my phone, place my head down and walk to the bathroom slowly. My feet now dry, the rest of my body slowly air drying off, I place a towel on the edge of the toilet seat to protect the coldness of the seat going onto my balls. I loosen the envelope with my finger and slowly take out the letter.

Dylan's Battle

Chapter Ten - Dylan 5:50pm

The room is silent, everything is silent, I can't see him, I can't hear him, all I see is this letter, all I can hear is the low hum of the light bulb just above my head.

I'm staring at her writing, not actually taking any of the words in, my world is blurry from the salty liquid bursting over my eyes. I take a deep breath in and prepare for what I feel will be my world crashing down, once again.

Dylan's Battle

To my darling boy Dylan,

I know this must be a scary time for you, just as much as it's a scary time for me. You know the doctors have said I only have 48 hours left now, but my body is telling me it's less than that, I am so weak and so tired. I fear my time in this world is going to come to an end sooner rather than later, and that's ok dylan. I feel like I need to write you this, so you can look back and re-read this when things are not going so well. Please don't be so hard on yourself when I am no longer here, it's not fair, I know it's not my darling boy, but you'll get through it, and remember I'll be there holding your hand in the hardest and darkest times. Make sure you look after Chloe too, she

Dylan's Battle

is a good girl, she's good for you Dylan, you're no good in your own company you know that. I'm so sorry I'm not going to be here to watch you grow up anymore, you're always going to be my baby grandson. I love you more than you'll ever understand, please be the person I know you can be. Sometimes life isn't always an easy roller coaster, but enjoy the ride Dylan because you never know how much time you have left.

I love you so much my darling boy, I'll always be here to watch you and protect you.

    I love you and I'll see you again one day

    Stay Strong, Stay Resilient, Be yourself always

    Nanny xxx

Chapter Eleven - UF 6PM

I'm watching Dylan's pathetic naked body, crying over that stupid fucking letter. I'm slowly, quietly whispering do it, do it do it. I see him getting agitated as I get louder, I see him looking at the letter, I see him looking at the broken piece of mirror. This is my fucking chance.

DO IT DYLAN, JUST FUCKING DO IT. YOU'VE ALREADY DISAPPOINTED YOUR NAN, SO CARRY ON BEING THE DISAPPOINTMENT.

FUCKING

DO IT

DYLAN

Dylan's Battle

Chapter Twelve - Dylan 6:03pm

I place the letter down, now slowly damp by the salty water, beaming from my eyes. I place my phone to the left playing Human by Cristina Perri on repeat, the only song I know that will keep me safe. I close my eyes and place my hands over my ears as I hear him shouting at me to do it. He's right though, I've disappointed nan, I am a disappointment, Chloe deserves better than me, I am the disappointment he's always told me I am, he was right, and I was wrong. I reach over to my right now, and pick up the cold sharp piece of mirror, I step into the bath and turn on the overhead shower, I run the hot water letting the heat inject its warmth into my body. The water swirls through my hair, trickling all the way down, until it escapes this reality through the drain. I pick up the

Dylan's Battle

sharp piece of mirror, letting the water bounce off the small amount of reflection that the mirror is. I know what is about to happen, I know what I'm about to do, I take a look around me, through the steam of the shower, I can't see him, I can't hear him, he must be proud of me.

Holding the piece of mirror I place the sharpest point onto the soft warm skin on my thigh. I close my eyes, focusing on the music, appreciating the obvious yet loudest silence from him. I press the mirror down onto my thigh slowly dragging it down, feeling the sensation of the warm blood trickle up, the burning sensation as the mirror splits the skin creating the newly acquired soon to be scars. I close my eyes, and repeat the process. It feels good to have this feeling, a different feeling, I feel pain, I feel the sensation of the mirror slicing the

Dylan's Battle

skin, I feel like I'm in control. The only thing I can control is when to stop; only I can control how deep to go. I feel the smallest amount of release and pressure leave my body..

I can smell the blood, the strong smell of iron, bouldering up my nose with so much force.
I slowly carve away at my thigh, zoning out not really knowing what I'm doing, but fully aware, when the mirror is connected to my skin, I'm creating a fresh wave of blood bubbling over what's just been opened. I look down and in some small way I get what I've always wanted on my thigh, my tattoo, because do you know what? I'm only human. I can see the words 'only human' forming in blood, as I look down on my thigh to see what other damage I've caused to myself.

Dylan's Battle

I notice I've quite literally made myself a blood bath. The now red water, escaping through the drain, I turn the shower off, step outside of the bath, and slowly pat myself dry.

I feel the cuts, red raw and stinging me, burning like nails scraping a black board, every time I bend my leg.

I feel the welts as my skin creases but it reminds me what I am, a fucking disappointment.

Once the blood eventually stops flowing and begins to clot, I walk to my room, bollock naked, and survey the scene.

I can hardly remember trashing my room like this, but who else was it going to be, I know I got angry, but this angry? Holy shit.

He was right once again.

You are weak. I am weak.

Dylan's Battle

You're a disappointment. I am disappointed.

You're worthless. I am worthless.

I pick up a pair of fresh boxers that have been launched to the opposite side of the room, I then wrap pieces of toilet roll around the cuts, to protect them. I'm not ashamed of them, I just need to look after them, they are a part of me, I'm a part of them. I wrap them up tightly, feeling the pressure, almost bursting the clotting wounds back open. I then place my boxers over the top for more pressure, more pain, more security, more protection. I move my attention to the left of me, I look at the broken mirror, I go towards it and move debris out of the way, just enough so I can sit in front of the shattered mirror. I place myself down, sitting opposite it, the pain from my ankle coming back as it is screaming up my leg as I place myself down, fucking thing, I forgot I fell on it. I

Dylan's Battle

no longer recognize myself. I'm unsure what is more broken, it's like a competition, what is the most fucked up piece in this room right now, the mirror or me.

I stare deep into my eyes, seeing all my thoughts whipping through my mind, they are flying around my head, too many to catch, an overwhelming amount of thoughts, too many to focus one into my mind, I see him also, standing behind me **hahahahahahaha.**

I can hear him laughing, I hear him mocking me. I look directly into his eyes, please go easy on me, I plead. I don't know if this is what can be classed as a psychotic episode, but I feel time, I feel it running through my fingers, yet I'm frozen in the position I am in. Unable to move, just feeling the time slipping away, I try to catch it to pull me back into my own reality, away from this hell hole but I'm trapped in a continuous loop of thoughts swarming through my mind.

hahahaha, his taunting, crushing laugh.

BOO

I'm out of his trance, I grab my phone. Fuck 3 hours have passed, I've stared into my broken self for 3 fucking hours straight. I've lost track of time, I couldn't hold onto the time I had, and now he has claimed 3 hours I'll never get back. I lie on the floor, noticing im covered in bugs, crawling all over my body, their little legs climbing behind my back, I'm shitting myself I stand up jumping trying to get the little bastards off me, but by the time I land on my feet they are gone, I know they was there, how can they just disappears, or is he just fucking with me. **Don't let the bed bugs bite Dylan.** I slowly rub my eyes and grab my phone to see Chloe had texted me over an hour ago. I'm so sorry Chloe **She doesn't deserve you, you fucked it all up DYLAN.**

ITS YOUR FUCKING FAULT NOT MINE, FUCK YOU.

BE QUIET DYLAN

I flinch as he shouts at me, covering my ears with my hands, closing my eyes, flashbacks of my childhood, where he has inserted himself into past memories slowly changing the narrative to one that suits him much better. The narrative where he has infected every inch of my life, just like a poison spreading through my bloodstream, oozing into every inch of me, mentally, physically, he is taking over me. I grab my phone to distract myself and open up the text from Chloe, feeling guilty everytime I see her name. Maybe she does deserve better than me.

> I love you Dylan, I don't know why I've got a bad feeling in my tummy, you know you can tell me anything no judgement here baby, I'm probably just over thinking but you have been a little distant recently, just want you to know I love you the mostest forever baby x

Dylan's Battle

I go to my call list, I see Chloe's name, I realise how much I've missed her today, I don't think I realise how much I actually need her.

Dylan's Battle

Chapter Thirteen - Dylan 9:25pm

I hit the call button, avoiding the big crack sprawling across the screen and before the first ring enters my ears, her voice fills my head, mind and soul.

I get butterflies instantly. **She hates you.** 'How are you feeling, baby?' Chloe said almost instantly in her most calmer and reassuring voice. 'I'm doing okay, I've just got a headache it's pounding harder than ever though' **you lying fucker, you're still lying to her after everything huh?** I can see him in the corner of my eye, laughing at me. I'm trying to have a conversation with the girl of my dreams, yet he is mocking me. How is this fair? **How are you going to tell her about all those fresh cuts and your pretty fucking picture sculpted into your skin?** I breathe in and out. 'I love you chloe, like really love you' I try and say this in my most reassuring voice, but can already tell this isn't really working while my voice is cracking, fucking typical. **HAHAHAHAHAHAHA.** I'm staring at him still laughing at me, he's bent over, slapping his knee like he's in fucking panto. Before I even realise Chloe has started talking again, I see red, I'm angry, the heat is blistering through my skin, surging out of my pores, leaking out of my cuts. 'WHY DON'T YOU JUST SHUT THE FUCK UP, YOU'RE MY FUCKING HEADACHE'

'What the fuck' I near Chloe's voice sounding almost just as broken. It streaks a dagger into my heart, **look what you've done now knobhead**. 'No not you baby, I'm so sorry, I was talking to the telly, it wouldn't turn off when I was pushing the button' I'm really reaching here scanning my brain for anything to get me out of this. It really wasn't meant for her. It was for him. The constant thing that's making my life unbearable, and now he's infecting the one thing in my life that's making life bearable. 'It's okay don't worry about it babe' Chloe says this while exhaling and staggering a breath. I need to leave this phone call pretty sharpish before I ruin this situation even more. ' Look baby, my head is killing me, I really need to just close my eyes and get more sleep, are you still coming tomorrow? I was thinking we could go to Nandos?' Chloe's silent tears falling down her cheeks are unbearably loud at this point 'Are you sure, you're okay baby, I won't be mad if you tell me, if you haven't been taking your medication, it's okay, we can sort it all out I promise babe' **lie to her, like you always do, lie to her, or I'll fucking hurt her** 'I've been taking them babe, I promise it's just a headache, more sleep, plenty of water, I'm sure I'll be fine' I say in the most pathetic exhausting sounding voice I've ever heard. 'I'm just worried about you dyl. Last time this happened, you did something stupid remember? I just want to make sure you're ok, we can get through everything together. Me and you forever remember?' 'I remember baby, I remember I'll see you tomorrow okay? I love you the mostest' As the words I love you fell through my mouth, something landed in my stomach, butterflies fluttering around, yet something felt so final about those words. I'm pretty sure the silence of Chloe's crying isn't so silent anymore, it's now her voice that is breaking, 'No, I love you the mostest baby, try and get some sleep baby, I'll be down as early as I can in the morning, 9am? I'll get the bus to get down earlier, But I'll text you as soon as I wake up, ok? Night I love you' **shes a fucking liar,**

Dylan's Battle

she wants you dead. Chloe practically said all this in one breath before gasping for another breath trying to stifle her cry. 'Night night baby, I love you even more the mostest, 9am sounds perfect, bye baby, night i love you the mostest forever'

 I get those final words out before hanging up, my chest heaving, my shoulders creating their own tsunami, as the salty water once again floods through my eyes.

Dylan's Battle

Chapter Fourteen - Chloe 10pm

I look at my phone to make sure the phone call is disconnected, I double check that my bedroom door is closed. I close my eyes placing my phone to the left of me, my stomach feels in knots, like I'm about to throw up, my head is orbiting different planets at insane speeds, I can't hold onto anything but mine and Dylan's memories, I'm so worried about him, my eyes release droplets of the tears before the wave comes, my face turns reds, my shoulders feels like they are experiencing a hurricane of their own, how can I help someone who doesn't want to tell me what's really going on? I knew I had a feeling this morning that something was off. Tomorrow we will be able to sit down and have an honest, genuine conversation. He just needs to be okay

Dylan's Battle

tonight, he said he's going to go to sleep now, I'll get there nice and early and I'll even stay a couple of nights to make sure he is taking his medication and keeping himself safe. I wipe my eyes, and a piece of snot that has apparently made an appearance as soon as I hear a knock on the bedroom door ' night chloe, I'll see you in the morning, do you need anything before I go to bed now?' 'No thank you nanny, night night' I say back trying to sound as composed as I possibly can be right now.
I pick my phone up, looking at the popsocket connected to my phone case, I smile as I see the selfie of me and Dylan at Thorpe Park, I smile even have a small chuckle, remembering all the time Dylan moaned that his feet was hurting him from queuing, moaning we had queued three hours for Saw the ride, when realistically it was only about forty-five minutes, we laughed for the next

thirty-five minutes at the fact only forty-five minutes had past. We went on the water ride. We got absolutely soaked, luckily it was the last ride of the day for us. I couldn't wait to get off the ride, but Dylan's eyes lit up; when the people asked if we wanted to go around again, how could I say no, when his eyes looked like someone just offered him a million pounds? We looked up, at the ride heading towards the peak of the ride, we were front row, and Dylan had both his hands in the air, he kept grabbing my hand, while my other hand was gripping onto the metal bar keeping us safe, I was laughing telling him to let go, so I can survive this wave all over again. I could hear Dylan laughing and screaming as we very quickly descended to the bottom of the ride. I saw the flash from the camera as the first spots of a wave hit us, before what felt like a hundred gallons of water landed

Dylan's Battle

over both of us, as Dylan was clapping and cheering, I was shivering yet seeing him so happy I couldn't help but clap and cheer with him. I held his hand, I gave him a kiss, I remember whispering in his ear, I love you so much. Dylan gave me one of his cheeky smiles and whispered back 'I love you the mostest'.

 After that we headed back to the shark cabins to dry off because we booked a room in the theme park. Dylan fell asleep in my arms, just as we were about to get ready to go out for food. I will never forget seeing Dylan sleeping with that precious smile spread across his face, it's a core memory that will be engraved into my mind forever.
I pick up my phone, go straight to Dylan's name in iMessage.

Dylan's Battle

I could tell him a million and one things right now, but I think he needs to hear one thing, maybe the most important thing, more than anything else.

I wipe the tears off my face as I type.

> If you've been struggling or feeling down lately, it's okay baby, we can sort it all out together tomorrow, we can have a proper chat, we can maybe sort a doctors appointment out, see if your medication needs readjusting, I just have a gut feeling, it's not just a headache and that's okay. I love you more than life itself Dylan, always and forever xxx

Dylan's Battle

I place my phone on the bedside table, still with this bad feeling in my stomach that there's something wrong, but I'm no good to Dylan if I'm no good tomorrow. I place my head on the pillow, drifting off to a dream where I know Dylan is well and healthy again. I go to sleep knowing tomorrow will be difficult but will do anything to make sure Dylan is happy. He is the love of my life, we've gotten through so much shit together, this is just another mountain we face, together as a team. I quickly pick my phone back up, I kiss the screen, I whisper goodnight, I then slowly drift off, leaving behind a difficult day.

Dylan's Battle

Chapter Fifteen - Dylan 10pm

Chloe's call screen disappeared, I went straight to the music app and did what I always do, make a playlist. I know exactly what I need.

1. Christina Perri - Human
2. Harry Styles - Fine Line
3. Christina Perri - Human
4. Taylor Swift - This Is Me Trying
5. Christina Perri - Human

I grab my headphones, I hit play, my mind absorbs the music, the instruments, the words. I hear vocals layered upon other vocals, I hear all the instruments individually, yet I hear them join the accompanying instruments. I can feel lyrics getting etched into my heart, body and soul. Just for this brief twenty minutes, the world is quiet. It

Dylan's Battle

feels like I'm hearing these songs for the first time. How many people would love to experience a song they fell in love with for the first time again? Listening to the song, feeling every word, connecting to every word, not knowing where the song is going, feeling the build up, until it hits the climax before slowly scaling back down. There is also a finality about them, I don't know why. Like I don't understand why there are tears brimming past my eyelids as the last song plays out. I pick my phone up and see Chloe has text me. I kiss my screensaver, the photo of me and Chloe, I download my playlist to play it offline. I drag the drop list menu down, and put my phone into aeroplane mode. I look up to him, standing in the corner of my room nodding, I whisper to him, cutting myself away from the rest of the world.

Dylan's Battle

Another tear is falling, just grazing my cheek as he says

good boy Dylan.

Dylan's Battle

Chapter Sixteen - UF 10:30pm

I need to surprise Dylan, I've been quiet for far too long, I need to push him to his limits, I need him to question what's real and what's not. I can see Dylan trying to prepare himself for me, but this is it, the final blow. It's time

To

Give

Him

Hell

DYLAN PEOPLE ARE COMING FOR YOU, THEY'RE GOING TO FUCKING KILL YOU, THEY'RE GOING TO TORTURE YOU, THEY

Dylan's Battle

WILL KILL CHLOE.

HAHAHAHAHA YOU HAVE TO DO THIS NOW, OR THEY WILL FUCKING KILL YOU

HAHAHAHAHA QUICK SOMEONE IS GOING TO KILL YOU, BEAT THEM DO IT DYLAN, I WILL FUCKING KILL YOU MYSELF IF YOU DONT DO IT.

IM NOT SCARED OF YOU DYLAN I WILL FUCK YOU UP.

HAHAHAHAHAHA AHHHHHH

DYLAN THIS WON'T END WELL FOR YOU DYLAN, HAHAHA IT'S TIME FOR YOU TO FUCKING DIE DYLAN YOU NEED TO DO MORE DAMAGE THAN THAT SHIT IN YOUR LEG DYLAN. FUCKING RUN AND DO IT!! NOW KILL

YOUR SELF DYLAN ITS THE ONLY WAY TO SAVE CHLOE. IF YOU'RE NOT FUCKING DEAD BY MIDNIGHT, CHLOE

Dylan's Battle

IS FUCKING DEAD

TAKING YOUR

PLACE INSTEAD

YOU SELFISH

FUCK

I watch Dylan take his earphones out, he lowers his head and sighs. He's staring right at me. I go behind his head and lean forward so he can feel my breath on him. I get closer and closer and then I scream

DO IT

DYLAN NOW

KILL

YOURSELF

DIE

Dylan's Battle

Chapter Seventeen - Dylan 11pm

I feel like I've been ambushed by thirteen thousand different voices, whizzing around my brain, slowly separating yet still in one piece somehow, I'm curled up in a ball, going back to the first position we all start in. The foetal position, whimpering like a 3 year old, scared of the monsters under the bed. The only difference here, my monster is real. WHY DON'T YOU JUST LEAVE ME ALONE I scream, **hahahaha** he's just laughing at me, he's mocking me, he doesn't give a single shit about me. I put my headphones back in, putting the volume to maximum, I know it won't work again but I need this peace while I do this. I can still see him staring at me; his mouth isn't moving, but I can still hear him. I know he isn't real, but he feels so real, I can see him, I can hear him, when will my torture end? **You know when it will end Dylan.** I stand up feeling defeated, my ankle feeling nothing now, but my not so fresh cuts now stinking from the pressure of my joggers on them, but that's good. They remind me of what's real and what's not real. I leave my bedroom, I walk down the stairs and go straight to my front door, **be careful dylan.** I unlock the front door, and stand out in the front garden, just in the front-garden with no top on, it's cold. I feel the chill chattering my bones, but at least it isn't raining anymore. I look around and there are no lights on, everyone is asleep in this dark cold lonely night. I let the cold air run down my throat and nostrils, as I close my eyes, sharp breath in, as the icy air runs throughout my veins. I do it again, sharp breath in, letting the cold take hold of my body, goosebumps travelling through-out,

Dylan's Battle

starting at my feet, climbing my body, until every goosebump was raised. I took one final deep breath in allowing my lungs the fresh air that it truly deserves. I walk back to my front door, into the house and stare at the view, in all the ugliness inside my head, it's truly beautiful to appreciate the small things in life, like the condensation coming out when I breathe, or the blades of grass surviving everyday when they have the pressure of several people trampling all over them, I see them moving in the wind and I guess I see this as them waving goodbye to me. I close the front door with a small smile where only the corner of my lips are raised, almost enough for a cheeky dimple to show. I walk to the table, almost everything I need is here, some paper, a blue inked pen, my tattoo drawing from earlier, and an envelope. I just need one more thing, I head into the kitchen I go into a draw and see exactly what I need **pick it up dylan, you know it's the right thing to do FUCKING PICK IT UP.** GIVE ME FUCKING CHANCE I shout while saliva is landing somewhere like a poisonous snake attacking. I found the knife I use to carve my roast meat for Sunday dinners. I even remember how much I bought it for, £3.50 on sale in Asda, always thought it was a fucking bargain. It does the job, but it has got its biggest job to come. I collect everything together and stand in the living room, I look around, I see a photo of me and Chloe from prom night. I walk towards it and feel the dryness of the wooden frame as I pick it up, I look into Chloe's eyes, beautiful and bright blue, taking in that infectious smile.

Dylan's Battle

I whisper I love you, and place the photo back, face down. I take a slow walk back upstairs unsure what's about to follow next.

Dylan's Battle

Chapter Eighteen - UF 11:15pm

What the fuck are you doing now Dylan, wasting MORE fucking oxygen, what stupid childish idea do you have now? You know what you have to do, to save Chloe, they are going to kill her, they are going to torture her. Then they will come after you. SO WHY DONT YOU JUST FUCKING KILL YOURSELF, THIS ISNT FUCKING FUNNY DYLAN THIS IS THE END OF EVERYTHING. SO JUST FUCKING KILL YOURSELF.

I watch Dylan standing frozen in the middle of his bedroom, I walk around him, watching him squirm, I do a lap around him, seeing his eyes well up, and his knees shaking. I stand in front, stare deep into his eyes, as he stares into mine, he slowly nods. I know my job is done. I lean forward again. I go straight to his ear so I know he can hear me, in my faintest voice I whisper,

 well done, now it's time to end it for yourself. Do it for Chloe.

Dylan's Battle

Chapter Nineteen - Dylan 11:25pm

I sit in the middle of my bedroom, feeling the calmest I've felt all day. It kind of feels like a euphoric feeling, I clear some debris that's scattered on my bedroom floor from the outburst earlier on. I grab a magazine, and place my piece of paper on top of it. He's standing in the corner agreeing I'm doing the right thing. I stare at the piece of paper which feels like hours, but really only a few minutes pass. Before I know it, everything is falling out of my mind, I'm writing secrets between me and her, I'm writing our love story.

I take a deep breath when I've finished writing. I've easily written 3 or 4 pages, double sided obviously. I don't know when but yet again another tear flew out of the nest, and it has saturated the last couple of words.

Dylan's Battle

I'm so sorry

I love you the mostest

Dyl xxx

I take the drawing of my tattoo that I drew earlier and place it in between the sheets of paper that's now covered in my handwriting. I slowly fold the paper in half, ever so careful not to crease the drawing, Chloe won't appreciate that. I place my letter and the drawing, into the envelope. I raise the envelope up to my tongue and slowly lick for it to stick, FUCKING typical, I let out a little giggle, a papercut on my tongue, the irony in that is practically uncanny. I seal the envelope, I flip the envelope frontwards and I write To Chloe. I place the letter on the bed.

Dylan's Battle

I slowly walk to the bathroom, my knife now in hand, I set the knife on the toilet seat, I start to run the bath. I take off my joggers so I'm just in my boxers, I walk back into my bedroom, taking in one last look, of all the memories scattered throughout the room. I see my letter, I see a ruined room. I leave the bedroom door open. I walk back into the bathroom, I close the door. I see him, nodding at me. **You're doing the right thing Dylan. I'm so proud of you. You've always known what you've had to do to protect Chloe.** I give him a brief smile, before turning my attention back to the bath, it's hot, just how I like it.

I take my phone out of aeroplane mode, go straight to my text's messages, I quickly re-read some silly old I love you texts and then I send one last text to Chloe.

Dylan's Battle

> **Goodnight Chloe, I love you the mostest ever infinity... I win xxx**

I put my phone back into aeroplane mode, I hit play on my playlist that I made earlier. I place the knife on the edge of the bath. I first place my feet in, feeling the heat climbing up my body, I then lower myself in, until my entire body is fully submerged, just leaving my shoulder and head out of the water. I feel the water go over the cuts I created a couple of hours ago, stinging with every second they are submerged in the hot water. I stare up at the ceiling, examining all the current thoughts in my head, yet there aren't any there. It's silent, he's there nodding, and smiling sweetly at me.

Dylan's Battle

I take a deep breath in, allowing my lungs to inhale some of the heat that's rising from the water. I let my breaths come out staggered, realising I think I am more apprehensive than scared. I give a small smile. **It's time Dylan.**

I know I whisper back to him.

I grab the knife, letting the sharpest point slice through the water. It seems too easy for the knife, it just glides disturbing any water in its path. The song came back on, it's time. Christina Perri's vocals filling the void in the bathroom, he's now sitting on the toilet, with a smile, just nodding and staring.

I place the knife point at the top of my forearm, I apply pressure, I feel the knife edge split the first bit of my skin, with all the remaining strength I have, I keep hold of the knife, forcing it down my arm, I feel the flesh splitting, being slicing open, letting the dark red blood flow freely. I don't actually feel anything until the knife's deadliest point hits the wrists, I feel snapping, I feel separation. My arm loses its strength and its grip, I watch the knife as it falls in slow motion, making its way to the bathroom floor. I hear the clattering as it hits with a thud. I look at the scene, I see the depth of the wound, I see what I've created, I see the blood pouring out, filling the bath up even quicker than the tap. As my heart rate starts to get faster, it makes the blood gush out quicker. I panic thinking what have I done? As time stands still I realise there is no need to panic, I am content. The deep slice is different shades of red, my head falls back too weak to support anything now, I look to my left **goodbye Dylan.**

Dylan's Battle

He disappears, I'm all alone, my eyes are getting heavier, my vision is getting darker, my breaths are getting shallower, I hear the music barely in the background. I close my eyes while I struggle to take another breath in
'I'm only human, and I bleed when I fall down'
My last breath is slowly taken, and my last breath is slowly escaping me, while my soul slips away.

Dylan's Battle

Chapter Twenty - Chloe 9am

First anniversary of Dylan's death

21st of September 2024

I slowly open my eyes, immediately my stomach is in knots, I feel my whole body shaking, knowing the day I have been dreading has finally arrived. I've spoken to my councillor for 6 months about this day, how would I ever get through it? I got her number, I can ring any time I know that, but how do I not relive that day again? Our texts, our phone calls. I go into my sock draw, I grab the envelope. The letter Dylan left me, the suicide note. I've never opened it, I've never had the heart or courage either. I look at his silly handwriting, a fresh wave goes over me, I'm not angry anymore, I don't feel as guilty anymore. The only thing I'm doing from now on, is start my grieving process properly instead of becoming so angry and scared. It's taken me a while to understand that all of these feelings are normal, and grieving is such a unique thing to every single person, no one knows how they are going to act until you're suddenly put into a horrible position where you lose someone you love so deeply. It has taken me a long time to forgive myself for not trusting my gut instinct and going straight to his house that day. Mum and Dad have been incredible, looking after me and allowing me to cry, scream, shout and vent when I need to. The funeral was such a horrible day that I can not let myself relive ever again. I can never fall back into that state of desperation again.

My eyes fall back onto the envelope.

I take a deep breath in, and open the letter.

Dylan's Battle

Dear Chloe,

The End

Dylan's Battle

Thank you's

Firstly I'd like to thank YOU, for actually purchasing and reading my book!!
Oh My God, I can't believe you've decided to have a look into Dylan's life. THANK YOU. I hope you enjoy/enjoyed this book that I've spent hours/days/months crying over, stressing over, smiling and laughing.
This has been an actually crazy journey getting here to where I am now. While I'm actually writing this, I'm supposed to be doing my final draft edits but I thought this would be WAY more fun!!

Lucy - My beautiful fianceè thank you so much for supporting me while I write this book. Thank you for letting me moan, thank you for letting me have the time to actually complete this journey. The next Nando's is on me. I love you so much x

Lucy Arthur - Thank you so FUCKING much!! You have been genuinely my biggest shoulder to cry on during all this, thank you for reading the really shit versions of this book, that no one will EVER see HAHAHA!! To what the book has finally become. This book is genuinely **our** book, thank you for dedicating your time to help me make this dream turn into a reality and this dream come true.

Dylan's Battle

Thank you to anyone who has ever watched one of my TikTok videos, liked/commented/followed my journey while I'm ranting or crying about this book.

Thank you to anyone who has ever asked me a question about the book, or asked when it's released!! (IT'S OUT NOW HOLY SHIT)

Basically just..

THANK YOU THANK YOU THANK YOU THANK YOU THANK YOU THANK YOU

You matter, your voice matters, your mental health matters. We need you here. We all love you here.

Check out my Tiktok to keep up to date:
@samipompadom
Or find my facebook author's page! Just search for Harry Mitchell on facebook pages!

Book 2 Chloe's Time - Coming 2024 Preorder now on Amazon!

Printed in Great Britain
by Amazon